THEN & NOW

CATONSVILLE

D1089527

OPPOSITE: ST. TIMOTHY'S SCHOOL FOR GIRLS, 1891. See page 74 for the history of St. Timothy's School for Girls. (Courtesy of the Catonsville Room.)

THEN & NOW

CATONSVILLE

Marsha Wight Wise

This book is dedicated to the memory of Bill Bates (1956–2010), author, friend, and mentor.

Copyright © 2010 by Marsha Wight Wise
ISBN 978-0-7385-8625-0

Library of Congress Control Number: 2010922961

Published by Arcadia Publishing
Charleston SC, Chicago IL, Portsmouth NH, San Francisco CA

Printed in the United States of America

For all general information contact Arcadia Publishing at:
Telephone 843-853-2070
Fax 843-853-0044
E-mail sales@arcadiapublishing.com
For customer service and orders:
Toll-Free 1-888-313-2665

Visit us on the Internet at www.arcadiapublishing.com

ON THE FRONT COVER: OLD SALEM LUTHERAN CHURCH, 701 INGLESIDE AVENUE, c. 1937. The church was dedicated on Sunday, June 16, 1850. On the next day, the following paragraph appeared in a Baltimore newspaper: "It is a very nice edifice, of Gothic style, surmounted by a pretty tower. The Rev. Benjamin Kurtz and the Rev. L. Van Bokkelen officiated during the day in German and English languages." It was placed on the National Register of Historical Places in 1977. (Then photograph courtesy of the Enoch Pratt Free Library; now photograph courtesy of the author.)

ON THE BACK COVER: THE SUMMIT, 10 STANLEY DRIVE. The Summit was originally built in the 1850s–1860s for Charles and Margaret Koefoed. Charles Koefoed, a Danish consul to the West Indies, died before the house's completion, and his wife, never having lived in it, sold it to James A. Gary. The 100-acre estate became Gary's summer home. The estate was sold in 1919 and subdivided into a middle-income housing community called Summit Park by Mohler Brothers Real Estate. The mansion was placed on the National Register of Historic Places in 1979. (Courtesy of the Catonsville Room.)

CONTENTS

Acknowledgments

My deep gratitude goes to my husband, John, and our sons, Matthew, Jared, and Jason, for their support and belief that their wife and mom can do anything. Thanks, guys!

I would like to thank the following individuals for their invaluable time and assistance while writing my first book, *Catonsville*, which led to the writing of this book: Jeff Korman, manager, Maryland department, Enoch Pratt Free Library; Maggie Schorr; Lisa Vicari, curator of the Catonsville Room; Jean S. Walsh; and Louis S. Diggs, author. I would also like to thank the generous individuals who opened their homes and shared their personal family histories, photographs, and collections with me, including Scott Trapnell Hilleary, William Hollifield, Antoinette Lawrence Hughes, Stephen Lackey, and Trip Riley.

To the best of my ability, I have attempted to ensure accuracy, given the antiquated and often obscure nature of the subject matter and materials.

Please visit me online at www.marshawightwise.com.

All modern images are courtesy of the author.

References

Boblitz, Katherine S. "Catonsville, Remarkable for its Natural Beauty." *The Baltimore Sun*, 4 June 1916.

Brinkmann, Walter. *Never-to-Be-Forgotten Tales of Catonsville*. Baltimore: Hoffman Brothers Company, 1942.

Diggs, Louis S. *It All Started on Winters Lane: A History of the Black Community in Catonsville, Maryland*. Baltimore: Upton Press, 1995.

Heidelbach, H. Ralph. *Catonsville's Churches and Schools before 1950*. Catonsville, MD: Self-published, 1988.

———. *Catonsville's Institutions before 1950*. Catonsville, MD: Self-published, 1988.

Orser, W. Edward and Joseph L. Arnold. *Catonsville, 1880 to 1940: From Village to Suburb*. Norfolk: The Donning Company, 1989.

INTRODUCTION

Happy 200th birthday, Catonsville! The year 2010 marks Catonsville's bicentennial. The birth of Catonsville began with Richard Caton and his wife, Mary "Polly" Carroll Caton, daughter of Declaration of Independence signer Charles Carroll. It was upon his land that Catonsville was built. Carroll sent his bankrupt son-in-law to manage the land he owned west of Baltimore City. The Catons built their home on the site that is now occupied by the Baltimore County Public Library. The development of the Frederick Turnpike further attracted growth to the area, and many more estates and farms began to cultivate the area. By 1880, it was the preferred summer retreat from the heat of Baltimore City for some of the area's most prosperous merchants. The completion of the Catonsville Short Line Railroad in 1884 made the burg attractive to middle-income families, and a diverse village was born.

In 2005, I wrote *Catonsville* as part of Arcadia Publishing's Images of America series. It was a fascinating subject to research, through which I met many interesting people with deep roots in Catonsville's history. This book could not have happened without their generosity in sharing their family photographs and stories.

Often when meeting readers of the Catonsville book I would be asked, "What's located there now?" or "Can you tell me where such-and-such place was located?" This book, I hope, will help answers those questions and many more.

I hope that you enjoy this tribute to Catonsville's rich history.

CHAPTER 1

HOME SWEET HOME

GRAY GABLES. This was the home of Charles Wacker and his family in Eden Terrace. The structure was demolished to make way for the Baltimore Beltway in the early 1960s. Wacker was a partner in the firm of Struven and Wacker, ships' chandlers, in the early 20th century. (Courtesy of the Catonsville Room.)

SITE OF CASTLE THUNDER, *C.* 1936. In 1907, the land was purchased and the house demolished by former Senator John Hubner to make way for a hotel. Hubner changed his plans and built a house for Arthur C. Montell, a cashier at the First National Bank in Catonsville. It was a two-and-one-half-story frame building with a shingled exterior, a slate roof, and porches. The house was razed in the 1960s, and currently the Baltimore County Library occupies the site. (Then photograph courtesy of the Enoch Pratt Free Library.)

119 SMITHWOOD AVENUE, SUMMER OF 1910. The stone used for the foundation of this house, built in 1905, was believed to have come from Castle Thunder. The small sign on the front of the house says "R. Bockmiller. Painter." Pictured here from left to right are Barbara Elizabeth (age 43), Leonard (age 2 months), Richard B. (age 1), and Richard R. Bockmiller (age 37). (Then photograph courtesy of the Catonsville Room.)

HOMEWOOD, 717 EDMONDSON AVENUE. Originally called Chestnut Grove until the chestnut tree blight in the 1800s, Homewood was built on 52 acres in the 1840s by Joseph P. Fusting. The home still stands and has been subdivided into two apartments. (Then photograph courtesy of the Catonsville Room.)

6 OAK GROVE AVENUE, BUILT 1909. August Scharf (born 1859), a tailor, immigrated to Maryland from Germany in 1884. The following year, he was able to send for his wife, Matilde (born 1855), and their infant daughter Helena (born 1885) to join him in Baltimore. They would go on to have five more children. By 1930, the Scarf family had moved to Oak Grove Avenue in Catonsville. At left is Helena Scharf, and at right is Elizabeth Scharf (born 1890). (Then photograph courtesy of Joseph Angelozzi.)

6 OAK GROVE AVENUE, BUILT 1921. This is the former home of Frederick (born 1899) and Anne Scharf. Frederick graduated from the University of Maryland Law School in 1923. He later became a judge and is reported to have died on the courthouse steps in October of 1978. (Then photograph courtesy of Joseph Angelozzi.)

HOME SWEET HOME

101 Oak Grove Avenue, Built 1909. This is the current home of Joseph Angelozzi. Joseph befriended the Scharf family as a young man. He had been orphaned as a child, and the unmarried sisters Helena (left), a former schoolteacher, and Elizabeth (right), a former Western Union operator, came to think of him as a son. On of his fondest memories of Elizabeth, whom he called mom, was the potato soup she would make for him in return for his help around the house. Joseph purchased from the family the three homes on Oak Grove Avenue. (Then photograph courtesy of Joseph Angelozzi.)

ARDEN. This home was built by Victor G. Bloede in 1898 at an estimated cost of $13,000. The home was the centerpiece of the Eden Terrace community that Bloede's Eden Construction Company developed in the late 1890s. The house burned in 1922. Bloede built a stucco house in 1924 to replace his lost Arden, but it did not come close to replacing its predecessor's beauty and splendor. Today the house has been abandoned and is at risk of being razed for new development. (Then photograph courtesy of the Catonsville Room.)

GRIMES HOME, 101 ARBUTUS AVENUE, *C.* 1898. This home, one of the first constructed in Eden Terrace, is on lot No. 20, located on the corner of Woodlawn and Arbutus Avenues. (Then photograph courtesy of the Catonsville Room.)

DUNMORE. Dunmore stood to the east of Eden Terrace and was built by W. J. H. Walters. The *Baltimore Sun*, on May 11, 1908, announced that the structure was to be the new home of the Pot and Kettle Club. A 1915 reference said it was the estate of Frank T. Kirby. The home was a large three-story Victorian with fretted decoration. The house was torn down in 1941, and the community also known as Dunmore was developed. (Then photograph courtesy of the Catonsville Room.)

115 Arbutus Avenue, c. 1927. The 1925 Diana Roadster was owned by J. Russell Riley. It is pictured in front of his grandparents' home. The porches have been enclosed since then by an owner desiring more interior space. (Then photograph courtesy of Trip Riley.)

SUCRO HOME, 13 WOODLAWN AVENUE, C. 1892.
This splendid Victorian, the first house constructed in Eden Terrace, was built for German immigrant George C. Sucro, manager of the Bartholomew Brewery. Pictured here are George C. and Elizabeth Sucro (seated on settee on left); son Fred (next to settee); daughter Jennie (seated center); daughter Antoinette (sitting in foreground on slope); and son William (seated at far right). The others in the photograph are unidentified. There are two servants standing on the porch who were both German immigrants. The house has been in the family continuously for 113 years. (Then photograph courtesy of Antoinette Lawrence Hughes.)

BEVERLY, 12 WOODLAWN AVENUE, c. 1893. This home was built by H. P. Hall and is one of the original homes in Eden Terrace. Antoinette Sucro Lawrence and her husband, Arthur, purchased the home in 1915 from the widowed Mrs. Hall. It was located directly across the avenue from her parents. In 1920, the Lawrence family sold the home to J. E. Downs and moved across the street to No. 13. (Then photograph courtesy of Antoinette Lawrence Hughes.)

FARMLANDS, 1948. In 1848, Gustav Lurman Sr. purchased the estate known as Bloomsbury Farms, restored its original name of Farmlands, and proceeded to make it a Maryland showplace. In 1948, after his death, Farmlands was sold to the board of education for the construction of Catonsville High School. The house was razed, and all that remains is the groundskeepers' cottage and many of the rare trees. (Then photograph by Virginia Duvall, courtesy of the Catonsville Room.)

Rolling Road Golf Club   Catonsville, Marylan

BLOOMSBURY, *c.* 1919. The home was built by Gustav Lurman Jr. in 1881 on land he inherited from his father. In 1916, the house was acquired as part of the new Rolling Road Golf Club. It was the earliest clubhouse, in continual use from 1919 to 1991, when the club razed the mansion after erecting the current brick clubhouse. (Then photograph courtesy of William Hollifield.)

HOME OF THEODOR LURMAN, 901 SOUTH ROLLING ROAD. A lawyer, Theodor Lurman owned several sections of the estate of his father, Gustav Lurman Sr., known as Farmlands, at different times. Pictured here is one of his homes. It was designed by architects J. A. and W. T. Wilson. Later the home became the Rolling Road School (for handicapped children), and it is now the offices of the board of education. (Then photograph courtesy of the Catonsville Room.)

BELLEVUE, 850 SOUTH ROLLING ROAD. The home was last owned by R. Howard Bland (1880–1959), Harvard Law School graduate and former president of the U.S. Fidelity and Guarantee Company. In 1930, he served as president of the Spring Grove Hospital Board of Managers. The Bland-Bryant Convalescent Building still bears his name. The home was razed preceding the purchase of the property by the YMCA to build its Western facility. (Then photograph courtesy of the Catonsville Room.)

OVERHILLS MANSION, 916 SOUTH ROLLING ROAD. This home was built in 1897 by Henry James as a wedding present for his son Norman and Norman's bride, Margie MacGill, the daughter of a Civil War doctor. Overhills is a showcase of imported and domestic woods, from the fruitwood and teak paneling in the ballroom (added in the 1920s) to the massive columns that support the portico. It is currently being operated as a meeting and wedding facility. (Then photograph courtesy of the Catonsville Room.)

WINDSOR FARM. Windsor Farm was originally owned by Col. Edward Dorsey, who, in 1701, built a two-story framed house. In 1793, the home was substantially enlarged. In 1802, the property was sold to Jean deRoyer Champayne, a Frenchman. Legend says that he and a manservant buried gold on the property, but it has never been found. The house was razed in the 1960s, and Westchester Elementary School was built on the back of the property. (Then photograph courtesy of the Catonsville Room.)

HILTON. The mansion was most likely constructed and named by John Buchanan, the landowner at the time, in the late 1820s. By 1842, the property, greatly reduced in size, was used as a summer home by Judge John Glenn. Today the home serves as the administrative building of Catonsville Community College. It was placed on the National Register of Historical Places in 1980. (Then photograph courtesy of the Catonsville Room.)

UPLANDS MANSION, 4501 OLD FREDERICK ROAD, *c.* **1940.** This was the spring home of Mary Sloane Frick Garrett Jacobs. She wintered at her home at 11 West Mount Vernon Place (now the Engineers Club) and summered in Newport, Rhode Island. Uplands originally was designed by William H. Reasin. It was remodeled to its present design by E. Francis Baldwin. Both Reasin and Baldwin were prominent 19th-century architects. Today it is home to the New Psalmist Baptist Church. (Then photograph courtesy of the Enoch Pratt Free Library.)

FAIRLEE, 10 SEMINOLE AVENUE. The house was built in 1897. It is believed to be the summer home of William Read, owner of the Read's Drugstore chain in Baltimore. It was later owned by F. Marion McComas, who sold the property to John Motsko in 1957. The house has had several subsequent owners and, as of this book's publication in 2010, is currently for sale. (Then photograph courtesy of the Catonsville Room.)

1000 Edmondson Avenue. This home was built in 1915 and was referenced on the deed as the Roth property. (Then photograph courtesy of the Catonsville Room.)

BEECHWOOD MANSION. This was the home of Maryland senator John Hubner, who moved to Catonsville in 1870 and who served in the House of Delegates and State Senate off and on between 1880 and 1910. He was an active real estate developer in Catonsville. Catonsville Presbyterian Church was built on the front lawn of the house in 1921, when it was owned by the Coblentz family. The house was razed in 1963 for an extension of the church. (Then photograph courtesy of the Catonsville Room.)

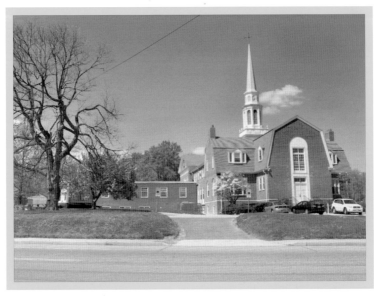

TANGLEWOOD. This was the home of Wesley M. Oler in 1894. Oler was in the ice and coal business or, as he liked to say, summer and winter. U.S. president Theodore Roosevelt was once a guest of the Olers. The house was razed in the 1930s for the development of the Tanglewood community, located south of Frederick Road and Maiden Choice Lane. (Then photograph courtesy of the Catonsville Room.)

EUREKA, C. 1894. Here is the home of Dr. Charles G. W. MacGill. Dr. MacGill, originally from Hagerstown, was the regimental surgeon of the famous 2nd Virginia Infantry, the "Stonewall Brigade," during the Civil War. The Italianate-style house underwent numerous renovations before achieving the appearance seen in this photograph. Located near Frederick Road and Bishop's Lane, the home was razed around 1950 and was replaced by a gas station. (Then photograph courtesy of the Catonsville Room.)

TOWER HILL. This was the residence of Henry James, president of Citizens National Bank and a lumber tycoon. Born in Truxton, New York, in 1821, James moved to Maryland as a young man. Besides his banking endeavors, he owned several lumber mills in Pennsylvania and Maryland. The estate was located on the northwest corner of Frederick and North Bend Roads. It was razed for the development of Jamestown Court. (Then photograph courtesy of the Catonsville Room.)

Waldeck, 736 Edmondson Avenue. This home was built in the 1870s by John Fefill and was called Stratford. The estate was purchased in 1877 as a summer home by Gustav and Auguste Gieske, who renamed it Waldeck, which means "woods corner." Gieske was a native of Oldenburg, Germany, and became a Baltimore tobacco dealer. Until recently, the structure was home to the Sterling-Ashton-Schwab Funeral Home. It sits on 6 acres of the original estate. (Then photograph courtesy of the Catonsville Room.)

OAKWOOD, 1300 SUMMIT AVENUE. In 1894, August H. Brinkmann, president of the Baltimore Corset and Novelty Works, purchased a large lot and started construction of a summer house the following year. Brinkmann hired Baltimore contractor Milton C. Davis to construct the three-story, frame, Queen Anne–style building at a cost of $20,000. It is shown here with its shutters closed for the winter. Today the house has been subdivided into a dozen apartments. (Then photograph courtesy of the Catonsville Room.)

NANCY'S FANCY, 5820 EDMONDSON AVENUE. Old land records show that William Logsdon Jr. owned a tract of land listed as "Nancy's Fancy on Hunting Ridge." Some time before 1880, Edward Spencer (1824–1883) and Anne Catherine "Braddie" Bradford Harrison Spencer (d. 1882) purchased the property. The Spencers died in the early 1880s of tuberculosis and left the care of their four children to an African American woman named Eliza Benson, who was a freed slave at the time and had once been owned by Braddie. Nan Hayden Agle, granddaughter of the Spencers, wrote a book about Eliza's life called *A Promise Is to Keep*. (Then photograph courtesy of the Catonsville Room.)

GLYNN TAFF, HOME OF REV. A. OPITZ, 5743 EDMONDSON AVENUE. This home was built in 1903. In 1918, Reverend Opitz purchased the house and opened a home for the aged and invalids. Today it is still an assisted living facility operating as Glynn Taff Assisted Living. (Then photograph courtesy of the Catonsville Room.)

HOME OF DR. WILLIAM SIMON, 311 INGLESIDE AVENUE, *c.* **1890.** Dr. Simon was a professor of chemistry at the University of Maryland school of pharmacy for 30 years. The school still gives out a prize in his name to a student who shows superior work in the field of biomedical chemistry. The once-grand Italianate-style mansion is currently home to the Forest Haven Nursing Home. (Then photograph courtesy of the Catonsville Room.)

BELLE GROVE, DARIUS CARPENTER HOWELL HOUSE, 12 HILLVIEW DRIVE, BUILT 1849. The estate ran from Frederick Road to Taylor's Lane. When bought by the Preston family around 1912, the estate comprised about 42 acres. Subsequently it was sold to George Kimberley and after that to a Miss Cole, who used the house and, by then, the much-reduced estate as a nursing home. Today it has been returned to use as a private home. (Then photograph courtesy of the Enoch Pratt Free Library.)

ROSEMONT, 28 MAPLE AVENUE, *C.* 1960. The original portion of this home was built in 1820. In the 1930s, the house lost its original gabled roof when it was burned during a bootlegging arrest in the Prohibition years. The bootleggers set the fire when Prohibition agents were reported to be coming to inspect the house. The current owners have restored the attic floor and found barrel-sized burn marks during the restoration. (Then photograph courtesy of the Catonsville Room.)

180 Oak Drive. This home was built in 1924 by Albert and Minerva Rolley. Albert was a sales manager for a wholesale electrical company. (Then photograph courtesy of Trip Riley.)

1111 Gary Drive. This home was built in 1948 by Joseph Riley. The home remains in the family as of 2010. (Then photograph courtesy of Trip Riley.)

204 AND 206 LOCUST DRIVE. The houses seen here are good examples of postwar housing constructed in 1947 by Marlen Realty. (Then photograph courtesy of Trip Riley.)

17 NORTH BEAUMONT AVENUE. The home is depicted here on a postcard dated February 17–22, 1911. This was the home of George Hardy, a widower, and his daughter Esther. They ran a boardinghouse here, as well. The date span may indicate a period that a border spent here. Today it is evident that the house was added onto after its original construction. (Then photograph courtesy of William Hollifield.)

10 Newbury Avenue. This home was built around 1860. At the time of the *c.* 1890 photograph, it was owned by the Jones family. Pictured here are Eda Jones (standing in the foreground) and Julie Jones (with the bicycle), along with the family's chickens, in the rear of the home. (Then photograph courtesy of the Catonsville Room.)

THE SUMMIT, 10 STANLEY DRIVE. The Summit was originally built in the 1850s or 1860s for Charles and Margaret Koefoed. Margaret Koefoed and the children lived in the gatehouse while waiting for the house's completion, which was halted during the Civil War. Charles Koefoed, a Danish consul to the West Indies, died before the house's completion. It was sold to James A. Gary, U.S. postmaster general. The mansion was placed on the National Register of Historic Places in 1979 and functions as an apartment house today. (Then photograph courtesy of the Catonsville Room.)

WHEELS OF COMMERCE

Frederick Avenue, looking West from Ingleside.   Catonsville, Md.

FREDERICK ROAD. Catonsville's main street is seen here looking west from Ingleside Avenue. Today the trolley cars have been replaced with buses and the horse and buggy with cars. The landscape has not changed much since the making of this postcard. (Then photograph courtesy of William Hollifield.)

ALBERT SMITH'S OFFICE AND HOME, 701 FREDERICK ROAD, c. 1881. Smith had his office for the Smith Steam Mill in the front rooms of his home, built in 1855. Through the years, it has had its facade drastically altered, and as of this book's publication in 2010, it is for sale. (Then photograph courtesy of the Catonsville Room.)

WHEELS OF COMMERCE

THE RAILROAD HOTEL, c. 1900. The hotel was located at Frederick Road and Egges Lane. It stood opposite the Catonsville Short Line Terminus. The hotel was sold in 1922 and was razed to make room for the new Catonsville firehouse, previously located at 22 Bloomsbury Avenue. (Then photograph courtesy of the Catonsville Room.)

CATONSVILLE HEALTH CENTER, 19 EGGES LANE. The first public health center in Catonsville was opened in 1926. Ethel Crosby, headmistress of the Crosby School on Beaumont Avenue, was a pioneer in public health work. Crosby spearheaded the opening of the center. A plaque honoring her can be seen on the center today, which continues to serve the people of Catonsville. (Then photograph courtesy of the Catonsville Room.)

CATONSVILLE GARDENS, 583 FREDERICK ROAD. The hotel served overnight guests as well as a being a stagecoach stop for those heading to Baltimore to the east and Ellicott City to the west. Through the years, the hostelry has had its facade drastically altered, and the structure current houses G. L. Shacks Grill. (Then photograph courtesy of the Catonsville Room.)

REMUS ADAMS'S BLACKSMITH SHOP. Catonsville has been home for numerous African American families both during and after the slavery years. Remus Adams, an African American man, ran a successful business during slavery. He owned a blacksmith shop at the intersection of Frederick Road and Bloomsbury Avenue. In 1909, the stone shop was razed, and the Catonsville High School, now the elementary school, was built. (Then photograph courtesy of the Catonsville Room.)

**F. A. Seicke Jr.,
715 Frederick Road,
1895.** This building housed
the telegraph office in the
1880s. According to the
signage, Seicke provided
"Telephones, Electric,
Gas Lighting, Call Bells,
Burglar Alarms, Door Bells
and Sign Painting." The
building was later used as
a doctor's office and was
torn down in the 1950s.
In 1970, the Catonsville
office of the Social Security
Administration was built
on this location. (Then
photograph courtesy of
the Catonsville Room.)

DR. LOUIS MATTFELDT, 908 FREDERICK ROAD, c. 1885. This was the first office and home of Dr. Mattfeldt. He would later move a few blocks down the street. Pictured here are Lem Schwinesberg (by the carriage); Dr. Mattfeldt; his wife, Wilhemina Schromsberg Mattfeldt (on porch); and an unidentified child and woman who were possibly Schwinesbergs. The law firm of McFarland and Masters, LLP, is the building's current resident. (Then photograph courtesy of the Catonsville Room.)

ALPHA THEATRE, 725 FREDERICK ROAD, *c.* 1944.
The Alpha Theatre opened on March 1, 1928, as a single-screen theater and seated more than 500 people. The Alpha closed in the 1960s. The building has been altered and used as various stores, but a check in the rear of the block reveals the theater, with the back twice as long as the other buildings. (Then photograph courtesy of the Catonsville Room.)

THE HEIDELBACH COMPANY, 720 FREDERICK ROAD, *c.* 1945. The Heidelbach's first grocery store was opened in 1882 and was located at 918 Frederick Road. In 1925, the company built and moved to this location. It was a grocery store chain of two, with the other store being located in Roland Park. The store closed in 1965. Plymouth Wallpapers currently occupies this building. (Then photograph courtesy of the Catonsville Room.)

A&P Super Market, March 1967. Located on the site of the former Raab residence, the A&P was in the 900 block of Frederick Road on the north side from the 1930s to the 1950s. (Then photograph courtesy of the Catonsville Room.)

UNION TRUST COMPANY AND IOOF HALL POSTCARD. The bank was built in 1922. The Independent Order of Odd Fellows Hall, constructed in 1909, can be seen behind the bank. (Then postcard courtesy of William Hollifield.)

HOUSES AT THE ENTRANCE TO THE CATONSVILLE WATER COMPANY, 6159 EDMONDSON AVENUE. The Catonsville Water Company was started by Victor Bloede to supply water to the Eden Terrace development in the 1880s. Using the same springs, the Catonsville Spring Water Company began in 1903. It produced carbonated beverages such as its own brand of ginger ale. The 1948 7-Up building still stands and serves as the Catonsville Transmission and Engine Repair shop. (Then photograph courtesy of the Catonsville Room.)

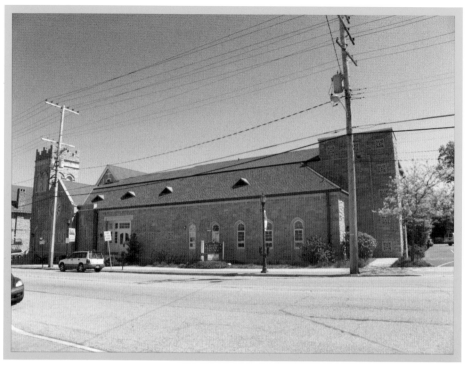

PETZOLD'S SALOON, 905 FREDERICK ROAD. The building was razed around 1900 to make room for Salem Evangelical Lutheran Church's expansion. (Then photograph courtesy of the Catonsville Room.)

SCHOTTA HOUSE, BOOT AND SHOEMAKERS, 825 FREDERICK ROAD. Richard and Mary Caton built this house around the end of the 19th century. The Catons had built the log cabin as a temporary home while Castle Thunder was being constructed farther west on Frederick Road. The building has gone through many renovations and is now home to the AWOL skateboard shop. (Then photograph courtesy of the Catonsville Room.)

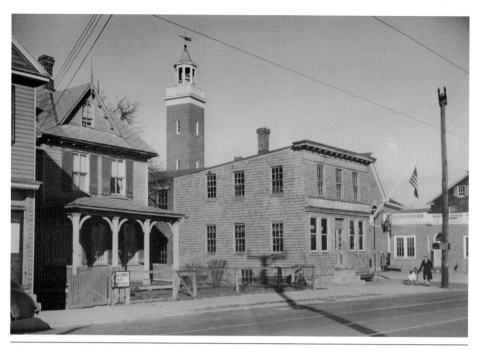

KALB POTTERY, 806 FREDERICK ROAD. The Kalb family owned a local pottery at this location until 1950. The Hamilton house on the left was razed around 1940, and the current home of Jennings Café, which still occupies the site, was built. The Jennings family has operated the restaurant since 1958. (Then photograph courtesy of the Catonsville Room.)

CATONSVILLE'S FIRST FIRE STATION, 22 BLOOMSBURY AVENUE. The fire station was located on Bloomsbury Avenue from 1889 to 1928. By 1908, Baltimore County's first motorized firefighting vehicles came to Catonsville. This postcard depicts two of the early fire trucks. The fire chief's car can be seen on the left. In 1928, the station moved to its current site on Frederick Road. The building has been greatly altered. (Then postcard courtesy of William Hollifield.)

Fire Department   Catonsville, Md.

CATONSVILLE POST OFFICE, 927 FREDERICK ROAD. The post office was at this location from 1922 to 1933. The current post office was built to the right of the office. Take note of the mansion behind the post office. It served as an apartment building at the time and was later torn down, as was this building. The site is now home to a gas station. (Then photograph courtesy of the Catonsville Room.)

RESIDENCE OF G. B. JOBSON. This home is a wonderful example of Queen Anne Victorian architecture that can still be found throughout Catonsville. The home stood on the land now occupied by the Catonsville Post Office at 1001 Frederick Road. (Then photograph courtesy of the Enoch Pratt Free Library.)

FIVE OAKS LODGE, 1920s. Originally a private home known as the Five Oaks estate, the lodge was built in 1850. The postcard reads, "Five Oaks Lodge, Eight Miles West of Baltimore, Maryland, on the National Highway, between Catonsville and Ellicott City." In the mid-1920s, the Rogers family, the owners at the time, began offering afternoon tea and light fare in the parlors and on the gracious porch. The Candle Light Inn continues the tradition today. (Then postcard courtesy of the author's collection.)

ELLERSLIE FARMS, c. 1919. The farm began in 1857 when the owner, Anthony Kennedy, purchased a Jersey cow named Alice Gray. Ellerslie was known for its purebred Jersey line. Kennedy died in 1894. His great-grandson C. Hughes Manley took over managing the farm. Manley died in 1918 at the National Dairy Show of Columbus, Ohio. The farm was located at 2501 Frederick Road and is currently home to the Patapsco Horse Center. (Then photograph courtesy of the author's collection.)

FREDERICK ROAD, LOOKING EAST. The landscape has not changed much except that the Ford Model Ts have been replaced with quite different automobiles. (Then photograph courtesy of William Hollifield.)

Frederick Avenue, looking East   Catonsville, Md.

EDUCATING THE MASSES

MANUAL LABOR SCHOOL FOR INDIGENT BOYS, c. 1890. Also known as the Arbutus Farm School, this school was started in 1840. The large stone building was constructed in 1860 and was destroyed by fire in 1916. The University of Maryland, Baltimore campus, now owns the land and has erected a plaque on the site. (Then photograph courtesy of the Catonsville Room.)

73

St. Timothy's School for Girls, 1891. St. Timothy's School for Girls began on Fusting Avenue in 1882. In the 1880s, several frame buildings were erected on the location of the former St. Timothy's Hall, and the girls' school moved there. It was an exclusive school established by Sallie and Polly Carter. In 1952, the school sold the property to St. Timothy's Church and moved to Stevenson, Maryland. The buildings were razed in 1967. (Then photograph courtesy of the Catonsville Room.)

CATONSVILLE HIGH SCHOOL, 106 BLOOMSBURY AVENUE. In 1925, the high school moved to the Bloomsbury Avenue location after the board of education purchased the property from the Catonsville Country Club. Students were immediately impressed with the wide hallways and bright classrooms. The high school moved to its current location on South Rolling Road in 1948. The school has since be reduced in size and currently houses the Bloomsbury Community Center. (Then photograph courtesy of the Enoch Pratt Free Library.)

First African American School in Catonsville, 100 Winters Lane, c. 1880. The community had a one-room school that was built shortly after the end of slavery in 1868 for African American children. That building was torn down to the foundation, and the Full Gospel Tabernacle Baptist Church was constructed on the foundation. In the early days, African American children were educated only to the sixth grade. (Then photograph courtesy of the Catonsville Room.)

OVERLEA COLLEGE, 108 DELREY AVENUE, BUILT 1860. Rev. Dr. George W. Eberling, pastor of Salem Lutheran Church, built the house for use as his home and as a school. It was designed to resemble a castle on the Rhine in Germany, from which Eberling had emigrated in 1853. The first two floors were used as the classroom and family quarters, with the third floor serving as the dormitory for the schoolboys. The school closed in 1895. It is a private residence today. (Then photograph courtesy of the Catonsville Room.)

CROSBY SCHOOL HOUSE, 20 NORTH BEAUMONT AVENUE. The school was founded in 1895 by Ethel Crosby in her home on Beaumont Avenue. A school room was built in 1914 and was enlarged in 1929. It burned down on April 8, 1976, during a two-alarm fire. The Kemp-Crosby house still stands as a private residence. (Then photograph courtesy of the Catonsville Room.)

EDUCATING THE MASSES

THE ROBERTS-BEACH SCHOOL FOR GIRLS, c. 1911. The school was located in a large frame house known as Searsleighs, built in 1898 as a home by Maj. John S. Gibbs. The school was founded in 1920 by Lucy George Roberts, Ph.D., and Sarah Morehouse Beach, Ph.D. The school closed in 1940 after a decline in enrollment that started during the Depression. In 1953, the house was subdivided into residential apartments. It accidentally caught fire and burned down. The Western School of Technology, located at 100 Kenmore Avenue, sits on the property today. (Then photograph courtesy of the Catonsville Room.)

EDUCATING THE MASSES

OUR LADY OF THE ANGELS CHAPEL OF ST. CHARLES SEMINARY. The chapel was erected in 1866. It is modeled after the Sainte-Chapelle in Paris, France. The property, excepting the chapel and the Sulpician community cemetery, was sold and converted into the Charlestown Retirement Community. (Then postcard courtesy of the author's collection.)

St. Charles College. The college was relocated to the seminary from Ellicott City after a fire in 1911 and was closed in 1977. The property was sold and converted into the Charlestown Retirement Community. It was placed on the National Register of Historical Places in 1983. (Then postcard courtesy of William Hollifield.)

St. Mark's School. CATONSVILLE, Md.

First St. Mark School, 20 Winters Lane. At the end of the 19th century, Catonsville built its first public school at this location. This building replaced a wooden structure in 1900. St. Mark Catholic Church purchased the Catonsville Public School building in 1910, when the school moved to its new home on Frederick Road, the current location of Catonsville Elementary School. St. Mark moved across the street in 1950 to its current location. (Then postcard courtesy of William Hollifield.)

EDUCATING THE MASSES

CHAPTER

4

WE WORSHIP TOGETHER

ATONSVILLE METHODIST CHURCH
FREDERICK AND MELVIN AVENUES
CATONSVILLE 28, MARYLAND

CATONSVILLE UNITED METHODIST CHURCH, 6 MELVIN AVENUE. Built in 1924 in the Gothic Revival style as a community house, the structure later became home to the church as well when plans to build a separate church did not come to fruition. At the rear is a brick addition from 1961. (Then postcard courtesy of William Hollifield.)

CATONSVILLE PRESBYTERIAN CHURCH, c. 1910. The church was built in 1881 and served as the house of worship for the Catonsville Presbyterian Church until 1922, when the congregation built and moved to its current location at Frederick Road and Beechwood Avenue. The first church was sold to Christadelphian Chapel in 1922. (Then postcard courtesy of William Hollifield.)

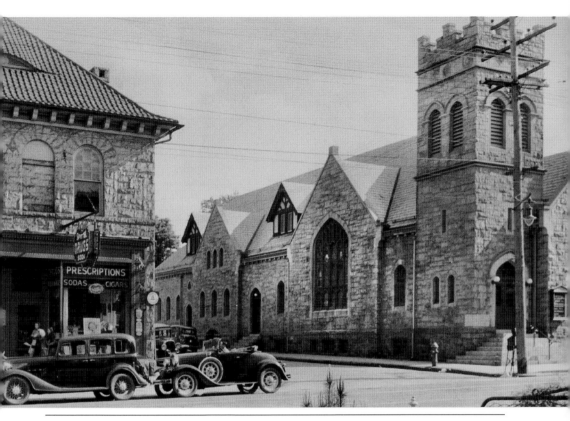

SALEM LUTHERAN CHURCH, MAY 1937. The original church on Ingleside Avenue was dedicated on Sunday, June 16, 1850. By 1901, the congregation had out grown its church, and it was decided to construct a new, larger one. The new church is located at Frederick Road and Newburg Avenue. (Then photograph courtesy of the Enoch Pratt Free Library.)

St. Timothy Episcopal Church.

CATONSVILLE, Md.

ST. TIMOTHY'S EPISCOPAL CHURCH, BUILT 1845. Catonsville's oldest church's congregation grew so rapidly that the original church was added onto in 1850. Additional expansions have been constructed since that time. The first rector was Rev. George F. Worthington. Judge John Glenn of Hilton was the primary benefactor of the church and was honored in death by his burial on the church's front lawn. (Then photograph courtesy of William Hollifield.)

CATONSVILLE UNITED METHODIST CHURCH, *c.* **1910.** The first Methodist minister in Catonsville began preaching in 1855 in private homes. By 1857, a stone church, called Providence Chapel, was erected on Bloomsbury Avenue on the current property of the Children's Home. The church pictured on this postcard was dedicated in 1887 on the corner of Frederick Road and Melvin Avenue. The parsonage, seen directly behind the church, was built in 1891. Both were razed in the 1920s. (Then postcard courtesy of William Hollifield.)

St. Mark Catholic Chapel, Built 1889. An altar of Italian marble was added in 1893, and frescoes were painted in 1905 by Louis Costaggini, son of the late Filippo Costaggini, who painted the frescoes in the Baltimore Cathedral. The old parsonage can be seen to the left. The larger church was constructed in 1950. (Then postcard courtesy of William Hollifield.)

St. Mark's Catholic Church   Catonsville, Maryland

PLACES OF INTEREST

PINE CREST SANITARIUM, *c.* 1910. The home was built in 1865 as a summer retreat known as Mount Brandon. In 1900, it was purchased by Anna A. Sieling (1867–1951) for the establishment of a private sanitarium named Pine Crest. It was lost to fire in 1967. In 1994, the land was given to the Maryland Environmental Trust. (Then photograph courtesy of Scott Trapnell Hilleary.)

GUNDRY SANITARIUM, 2 NORTH WICKHAM ROAD. The house, originally named Athol, was built by Charles Baker in 1880. In 1900, Dr. Alfred Gundry purchased the house and opened a private sanitarium for the care of nervous disorders of women that required treatment and rest away from home. It continued to function as a sanitarium until 2000. (Then photograph courtesy of the Catonsville Room.)

RICHARD GUNDY HOUSE, HARLEM LODGE, 327 HARLEM LANE. In 1891, Dr. Richard Gundy Jr. purchased a home formerly known as Maple Woods that was built in 1831. In it Gundy created a private sanitarium. The home was razed for the development of Maple Woods, a planned community. This building, most likely an outbuilding, is all that remains of the original estate. (Then photograph courtesy of the author's collection.)

The Richard Gundry Home, Harlem Lodge, Catonsville, Md.

GENERAL GERMAN ORPHAN HOME. The orphanage was founded in 1863 for children of German descent orphaned by the Civil War. In 1919, the General German Orphan Association purchased Talbot J. Albert's Belmont estate in Catonsville. The orphanage was moved from Baltimore City to its homier cottage-setting campus on Bloomsbury Avenue. The organization was renamed the Children's Home in 1985 and is in operation today. (Then postcard courtesy of William Hollifield.)

Administration Building, General German Orphan Home   Catonsville, Maryla

SPRING GROVE HOSPITAL. The hospital was founded in 1797 by Jeremiah Yellott, who established what was called a retreat for ailing mariners in Baltimore. The hospital was moved to Catonsville in 1872. The historical image is of the building known as the "Old Main," which was demolished in 1964. The modern image is of the Foster Clinic, awaiting restoration. (Then photograph courtesy of the Catonsville Room.)

Reservoir and Stand Pipe.   CATONSVILLE, Md.

RESERVOIR AND STAND PIPE, MELVIN AVENUE. In 1894, the Catonsville Water Company constructed a reservoir with a capacity of six million gallons. When completed, it was enclosed by an iron fence and had a fountain in the center. In little time, the reservoir began to leak on account of several muskrat holes. In 1937, the current water tower was constructed to replace the reservoir. The water tower is a domed structure built of a buff brick with limestone Art Deco–style trimmings. (Then postcard courtesy of William Hollifield.)

PENTHOUSE. Catonsville's charm as a wonderful place to make a home is not exclusive to humans. In 1935, this osprey, much to the chagrin of the telephone and power companies, made its home atop a utility pole. (Then photograph courtesy of the author's collection.)

www.arcadiapublishing.com

Discover books about the town where you grew up, the cities where your friends and families live, the town where your parents met, or even that retirement spot you've been dreaming about. Our Web site provides history lovers with exclusive deals, advanced notification about new titles, e-mail alerts of author events, and much more.

MADE IN THE USA

Arcadia Publishing, the leading local history publisher in the United States, is committed to making history accessible and meaningful through publishing books that celebrate and preserve the heritage of America's people and places. Consistent with our mission to preserve history on a local level, this book was printed in South Carolina on American-made paper and manufactured entirely in the United States.

This book carries the accredited Forest Stewardship Council (FSC) label and is printed on 100 percent FSC-certified paper. Products carrying the FSC label are independently certified to assure consumers that they come from forests that are managed to meet the social, economic, and ecological needs of present and future generations.

FSC
Mixed Sources
Product group from well-managed
forests and other controlled sources

Cert no. SW-COC-001530
www.fsc.org
© 1996 Forest Stewardship Council

Find Your Place in History.